The Boy Who Refused To Say, "I Can't!" My Journey. My Dreams.

By

Jesse "JB" Bradford

The Boy Who Refused To Say "I Can't"

Cover Designs by
Barron Steward
www.barronsteward.com

For booking information please contact Marie Bradford at glvmr21@hotmail.com.

ISBN: 978-0-9800071-2-1
To order additional copies, please visit
www.amazon.com Keyword: Jesse L. Bradford

Editorial consideration provided by
Coffeedreamz Ink, LLC

Dedication

This book is dedicated to my mother who I wish I had a chance to get to know, my father, and my sister, Evelyn, who never had a chance to reach their full potential; to my family and friends who supported me during my illnesses when I needed it most—Joyce, Marie, Michelle, Yolonda, Andre', Merlin, Nicky, Mart, Gwen, Minnie, Roy, Gean, Sharon, Stuart, and Juice; and to Morris Bisker and Vernon Coleman who gave me an opportunity I might not have had, otherwise, to grow and excel.

ROOTS & BRADFORD BRANCHES

**Blanch Bradford – My Mother
May 26, 1910 – December 17, 1940**

CHAPTER 1

I've had my share.

The face of Franklinton, North Carolina has changed slightly over the years. The town has a web site with a tagline that reads: "Small town, home town, your town". There are smiling black faces at the sheriff's retirement party and some of the boys in blue look like they could be distant cousins of mine. Other than that, today's Franklinton is pretty much the same as it was 58 years ago when I left at the age of 15. It still has a two-block downtown area and two traffic lights.

I'm a country boy, and like so many before me, I was delivered by a mid-wife on May 24, 1936. My mother, Blanch Bradford, died when I was four years old after a long battle with tuberculosis. I have very few memories of my mother, but I later acquired a black and white photograph of her from my older sister, Evelyn. It was almost like an illustration, but there was depth. It was almost three-dimensional.

Before my mother died, she gave birth to six children; therefore, I had five other siblings. Evelyn was six years old; Shirley Jean was two years old; Preston was 10 years old; and Percy was eight years old. My younger sister, Joyce, was a newborn – she was eight months old. After my mother died, caring for us and working in the fields became a challenge for my father.

My father was a sharecropper, a person who enters into a contract with a landowner to farm the land. The sharecropper pays a portion or share of the produce as rent to the landowner. My father did what he could for our family, but we were poor and could barely afford the basic necessities of life. Being a single dad was tough for my father, and my father's mother-in-law had a problem with him keeping us by himself.

Joyce was three years old by this time, and my grandmother was convinced my father was in no position to care for us. She got social services involved. My grandmother gave social services the impres-sion my father was unfit, and they should take us away from him. My grandmother had no desire to take care of us herself; she simply didn't want my father to have us just because she didn't like him. She didn't like my father because she thought he had been unfaithful to my mother while she was ill. However, my father would not give us up. So, Evelyn, Shirley Jean and I were sent to live with my father's mother in Youngsville, North Carolina. That was about 10 miles southeast of Franklinton. He sent Joyce to live with his sister, Estelle Neal. Percy and Preston, stayed with my father to help him work the farm.

When I went to live with my grandmother, Alverater Bradford, I spent a lot of time with my great grandmother. Her name was Millie Ann. Grandma Alverater had so many responsibilities caring for the home and making ends meet, that she didn't have time to build a solid relationship with us. Therefore, I spent more time with Great Grandma Millie Ann than I did with my grandmother. My great grandmother was part American Indian. She would tell me stories about her family. She said there were times that they would dance to cure certain illnesses and run ghosts away. Many of the things that she told me, I still remember.

Great grandma Millie Ann emphasized how important it was to stick together as a family. To illustrate the importance of family, she took one number two pencil and broke it. Then she took five number two pencils and put them together and tried to break them apart; she could not break them as a group. She said always stick together with your family because if you are united, you have strength.

At the age of 90, she still worked in the cotton fields. I think this is when I learned that hard work pays off, and it will keep you in good physical condition. Great Grandma Millie Ann lived to be 106 years old.

I later learned how to extend resources from my grandmother. She was great at "stretching" food so that all of us could eat. Grandma Alverater would add milk to the eggs to make a larger quantity. When we did not have enough clothes to wear, she would ask her friends for their hand-me-downs.

We went to school clean and happy despite the lack of financial resources. My grandmother's resourcefulness taught me how to enjoy life regardless of what you do or do not have. I played marbles, horse shoes, and baseball. When I got bored with those activities, I made my own recreation. I wanted to ride a bike, but didn't have one. So I used my resources to get one.

My first bike was not new. It wasn't shiny with all the bells and whistles. All that mattered was I could ride it, and it was mine. If I wanted to ride on the country roads, I had to make my own bike and built it from junk yard parts. Even though I had a bike, it could only accommodate one person comfortably. So getting to school required me and my siblings to travel the best way we knew how. The trip was 10 miles each way. Since there were no buses to take colored children to school, we walked. Riding the bus was a privilege for white children.

We walked in the burning sun, the cold rain, the hitting sleet, and the unforgiving snow. When the buses drove by us, the white children would throw things out of the window at us. As much as I wanted to fight back, I couldn't. The rules of the South would order me to be killed if I did.

Not only did I have to silently fight racism, I also had to defend myself against the neighborhood bully, JE. Since my older sister was a large girl, she would beat him up for me. Then one day, I told our Grandma Alverater she was fighting, and Evelyn got a good 'ole southern *whoopin'*. When the smoke cleared from her behind, Evelyn told me I'd have to fight my battles on my own from then on. Her bodyguard days were done, and I had to learn to fend for myself. I learned my lesson from my sister. It was simple, really. *Don't rat on the person doing the biting for you. You'll get bit.*

I quickly built up the courage to fight for myself. JE and I fought constantly. We shot spit balls at each other in the classroom. We threw things at each other; we were very disruptive. One day our teacher grew tired of our antics. She took a belt and tied our left hands together and said, "Go for it." JE and I fought and fought until we couldn't fight anymore. Nobody won. Since there was never a clear winner in our fights, we asked, "What's the point?" After a while JE and I became friends. I'm glad we did, because he later drowned, and it was only then I learned his last name. JE Garner was how he was listed in the newspaper's obituary section.

Although I didn't have much growing up, I was sent angels throughout my life. Being friends with Otis Black earned me a new wardrobe. Otis was my classmate in elementary school. His grandmother bought me a suit. It was blue, and it was my first. I was so very proud of the suit; I strutted around like the old

NBC peacock. That was one of the happier moments in my life.

When I was old enough to help my father in the fields, I was sent back to Franklinton to help him out. Evelyn went back with me.

Evelyn was a very important person in my life. Although she was only two years older than me, she was the woman of the house—Evelyn was 12 years old and I was 10 years old. She cooked for me and my two brothers, washed our clothes, and worked in the field too.

Evelyn was tough. While she didn't show much expression, she held strong emotions. You could hear them through her words and the tone of her voice. For example, there were only four biscuits to be shared by the whole family, and my share was one, but I took two. She made me put one back; I knew not to cross her again.

My father did not eat his meals with us. He went to his girlfriend's house to eat. This made Evelyn very angry. She continued to be angry with him throughout most of her life and found it hard to forgive him.

My father married a second wife, Christine Perry,

about six years after my mother died. They had two children together, Arthur and Mack. The marriage lasted only two years. Christine left and moved to New Jersey and took my two brothers, Arthur and Mack, with her.

One of the harsh realities of being poor is that work came before school. I attended B.F. Person School in Franklinton when I could. In preparation for the annual harvest, my father would take me out of school to farm. Luckily, Helen Jones, a girl from school, committed to help me with my school work. She would bring the homework to me and help me so I could keep up with the class. I passed every year, even after working long days from sun up until sun down for five years.

It was my job to help my father count the supplies that were delivered to the farm. One day we went to the owner to make the final payment on our bill. We learned the owner had charged us for all of the supplies, rather than for 50% of the supplies as agreed.

When we asked him about the charges, he became angry and dug into us like we were the dirt of the earth.

"Nigger, you do the work, and I will keep up with the money," the land owner said.

My father only had a third grade education, so he didn't challenge him any further. If he had done so, it would have been very difficult for my father to enter into another sharecropping contract with a different farmer. The white farmer would have blocked his opportunities with all of the farmers in the area by blacklisting him.

I, on the other hand, took my first step toward civil rights and challenged the land owner and told him, "That's not right!" By this time, I was tired of stones being thrown and people treating my family any way they pleased. To protect me, my father made me leave the land owner's office. I knew, at this point, there was something in me that desired more than sharecropping. There had to be a better way to make a living.

I let the air cool and then went to my father, not as his son, but as a man who had made up his mind to search for more because I wanted more, and I wanted a better life for myself. I had my share of being treated like a second class citizen. Enough was enough.

"Dad, I will help you get the crops harvested, and then I am leaving town," I told my father.

14

"Boy, you are only 15 years old. You can't leave home. There is no work for a 15 year old," he said, with a confused look on his face.

"Thanks for your concern, Dad, but I want to try," I said firmly. My father smiled and walked away knowing that, with a limited education at 15 years old, I couldn't survive. He seemed convinced I could not make it on my own.

After the crops were harvested, I went to the fields and picked the scrap cotton. Then I went to the mill and sold what I picked for $30. My wheels were now in mottion.

Before leaving Franklinton, I had to tell the only person whose feelings truly mattered to me--Evelyn. When I gave her the news, she was sad, but she supported me anyway. I went to town, along with two other cousins, and bought a bus ticket. I was on the next thing smoking out of Franklinton.

CHAPTER 2

Goodbye Franklinton!

My father's greatest fears were not being able to feed his children, but losing one of his sons to racial violence and not being able to properly educate his children. His fears were real and well founded. They were also fears I shared as well. Part of my reason for leaving Franklinton was to protect my future and the future of my children yet to come. I inherited my father's strong work ethic, even if my job was to mop floors.

The bus was scheduled to leave for Washington, D.C. at 7 p.m. and 11 p.m. My cousins, Carlton and James, decided to take the trip north with me. Our tickets were $12 each. By the time my father got home from the fields, I was gone. Since there weren't many transportation options out of town, I could only be one place, the bus depot. We saw my dad's red Ford parked outside the depot, but he did not see us. He stood around for a while so we couldn't make the 7 p.m. bus. We were able to slip by my dad and make our way to a nearby pool hall in a very discrete location, the alley around the corner from the depot. I set a budget for my trip and decided to spend only $3 while I was at the pool hall. We stayed there hoping my dad would be gone by the time the 11 o'clock bus arrived. Like clockwork, Dad grew tired and left. I got on the bus and headed for DC. With only $15 in my pocket, a one way ticket, one suit, two pair of pants, two shirts, and one pair of shoes in my shopping bag, I was on my way to the big city with big dreams. I was so nervous. I kept looking out the window to see if Dad was following the bus. He wasn't.

It was going to be a long journey to success, but I was willing to go all the way. After we arrived in Richmond, VA, I felt pretty safe and slept through the rest of the trip.

Even though my escape to DC would afford me opportunities, we were still living in segregated times. I had to follow the race rules, written and unwritten. Because we were colored, like most familiar stories about segregation, we were not allowed to eat at restaurant counters or sit with whites in public places.

We had to get our meals from the back of the bus stations in Richmond, Virginia and when we arrived in Washington, D.C.

While James and Carlton had a few hundred dollars between them, I had to stretch my money. They feasted on bacon, eggs, hash browns, and juice. I ate a hotdog and coffee for each meal. I wasn't envious of what they were able to buy. I knew a day would come when I could eat a big meal without worrying about the bill. I was confident in my future.

We arrived in Washington, D.C. at 7 a.m. the next morning. After eating at the depot in The district, my cousins and I caught a cab to Carlton's aunt's house. She lived at 602 2nd Street, N.E. near what is now Capitol Hill. We stayed overnight, sleeping on the floor. The very next morning, we got up and searched for a job and a room to rent. There were no online job sites or job fairs for colored men looking for work during this time period. We did it the old fashioned way; we went to a public unemployment office located at 5th and K Streets, N.W. At the unemployment office, I saw an old friend from Franklinton, Lawrence Spivey. He took us to a boarding house where we could rent a room at 930 P

Street, N.W.; we slept three to a room. It cost $6.25 a week per person to stay there.

The next morning, Lawrence came by the house to tell me his old employer, at a tea room, called him back to work. Lawrence cut a deal with his supervisor.

"If you hire my friend, I'll take my vacation and train him how to use the dishwasher," Lawrence said to his supervisor. His supervisor agreed; It was a done deal.

I had a job at a tea room at the intersection of 7th Street and Massachusetts Avenue, N.W. Within my first 24 hours as a Washingtonian, I had a job and a place to live. I had to add a year to my age just in case he wanted to deny me the job because I was 15. The legal working age, at that time, was 16 years old.

As a dishwasher, I was paid $27 a week, plus food. Even though I didn't get paid a lot of money, I was guaranteed a hot meal. When I started working, it was the first full hot meal I had in two weeks. I looked down at my plate and thought I had hit the jackpot. No more hotdogs and coffee for me.

Just as soon as the good times rolled around they got shaken up with sad news. I had been at work for only two days when I received word my oldest brother, Preston, died. James' mother called us with the news.

Preston had been sick with rheumatic fever. He was only 22 years old. I didn't have any money saved to make it back home. Even if I did, I risked losing the room my cousins and I were renting because neither Carlton nor James had jobs. All the money they started out with was spent on those full course meals and fun times in a new city.

My father did not know where I was; going home would jeopardize my plans to make a better living for myself. I feared my father would not let me leave Franklinton again. I wish circumstances could have been different, because I still live with the regret of not paying my respects to Preston. From time to time, I still feel like crying. With a heavy heart, I did not go to my brother's funeral.

In my new role as a big city dreamer, I had to make grown up choices---pay rent, buy groceries for three people for two months, and look for another job on my days off. Making difficult choices had a price. Since I wasn't going back to Franklinton to live, I would pay the cost of not losing my freedom."

Dad, Evelyn, and Me
Approximately 1955 during a visit to Franklinton

CHAPTER 3

"I don't have pets."

Although I was making strides toward my new life in The district, I began to worry about my father. I reached out to him and tried to get him to move to Washington, D.C. to stay with me. My first attempt was unsuccessful.

By 1953, I bought a car. Lawrence Spivey's uncle had originally got it for him under one condition. Lawrence had to pay the car note. Lawrence didn't keep up his end of the bargain, and I became the owner of a 1946 Buick. Having a car afforded me the opportunity to visit my family back in Franklinton more often. In fact, I made it my business to head home one or two weekends each year.

I had a few buddies who would ride to North Carolina with me. I had one rule: when it's time to go it's time to go. One buddy called my bluff and tested the theory one too many times. I needed to get back to The district at a decent time so I could make it to work on time. He wasn't at the meeting spot at the designated time. Needless to say, Washington, D.C. seemed really far from Franklinton when he realized we had left him.

The first lady I dated after moving to The district was Shirley Dean. She was very sweet and had a kind spirit. Shirley was great company in my travels back to North Carolina; we had a lot of fun. When I decided to get married, my family just knew it was going to be Shirley because we spent so much time together.

On Friday, December 24, 1954, I broke the news to Shirley; I was going to be married the next morning to someone else, Juanita Quarles. I could only imagine the hurt she felt. Without going into detail, I recognize that moment as the worst thing I had ever done and vowed to always be open, honest, and forthcoming about my feelings with people. I promised to always tell people the truth and lay my cards on the table, even if they don't like the hand I dealt them.

After my marriage to Juanita, I visited as often as I could with Evelyn and my father. We would often have our *"remember when"* conversations. While I was building a family with my wife, Dad was busy getting over his second wife leaving him. How did he cope? He fell for a younger woman---she was about 20 years younger than my father. He moved in with the lady and her daughter after all of us were grown. The relationship didn't last and my father later moved in to live with his sister. All of us were building our own families in different places, so it only made sense for him to be with someone he trusted.

While my life was not perfect, I had a new perspective on my future compared to my past while making plans in my present. I wanted my father to have a taste of life beyond the South, so I invited him to stay with me, my wife and children in DC.

My father accepted the invitation this time, but I soon realized how much of a homebody he had become. He was more interested in staying inside than exploring the city. He didn't like to go out a lot, and only stayed with me for one month in 1960. He missed North Carolina, so I took him back to live with his sister.

Aside from my yearly visits, I didn't see my father much. Our bond was strong enough, and our love for each other was unspoken. So I didn't have any regrets when a new year brought sad news. One day, my father was sitting by a fireplace and died from a heart attack.

The family waited for me to arrive before moving forward with funeral plans. When his second wife learned of his death, she came back to North Carolina. I thought she had come back for my father's funeral; but I later learned she came just to get the documents needed to collect his life insurance. She went to the funeral home, obtained my father's death certificate, and then went back to Jersey.

Although my father didn't favor one child over another, my siblings thought of me as "Daddy's pet". Therefore, when my stepmother took all of the insurance money, I was on the front line to take care of the arrangements. I was honored to be in a position to pay for the funeral.

My father never told me he was proud of me for taking a leap of faith to find a better life outside of Franklinton. His eyes spoke for his heart. Once he found out I was doing alright, he let that part of our history rest. So on January 2, 1964, the Lord let my father rest. He was 55 years old.

Evelyn Montague – My Older Sister
January 18, 1934 – August 14, 2002

CHAPTER 4

Passing the Torch

I found comfort knowing Evelyn was not alone after my father died. Five years prior to my father's death, Evelyn married Thomas Montague and started a family. They had two boys---Dexter and Mart.

Since Juanita and I celebrated our anniversary on Christmas Day and our family was growing, we spent Christmas Day in DC, and then I traveled to Franklinton on December 26, alone. Unfortunately, my wife didn't want to accompany me on the trips to visit Evelyn's family and my Aunt Savannah, an aunt I had grown very close to over the years. This became an annual tradition for me. In between my visits to North Carolina, it was customary for Evelyn and me to talk every Sunday.

I found joy in watching my nephews grow up. Dexter was always excited about seeing what kind of car I owned. When he was of driving age, I turned over the keys so he could show off the ride to the guys and girls in the neighborhood. Mart took a strong interest in finance and business. He was a nephew after my own heart. We spent hours upon hours talking about money matters. I was able to pass along my torch of wisdom regarding responsible spending and saving. I admired Mart's ambition and drive; he reminded me of myself when I was growing up. He often wanted to stay a step ahead and planned diligently for his future.

He once told me he wanted to buy his mother a house. When he got older, he found a house at a good price, and he had to make a commitment quickly in order to purchase it. He was going to use his bonus check to buy the house, but he was not scheduled to receive it until a month later. He only had a week to put a contract on the home and needed $10,000 to close the deal.

Because Mart had proved that he was a responsible young man and I was financially able to help him, I loaned him the money. Mart bought the house for his parents according to plan. A month later, Mart repaid his debt to me.

Evelyn and Thomas lived in the house their son purchased for them until their death. Evelyn died in 2002 and Thomas died in 2004. I was glad I was able to help Mart make a dream come true while his parents were alive.

For several months after Evelyn's death, I picked up the phone on Sundays and began dialing her phone number only to be saddened with disappointment that I couldn't speak to the only woman who was more like a mother than a big sister. She did, however, leave a legacy behind to remind me of her strength, her boys.

Percy (L) and JB (R) standing with Joyce (C) on her wedding day (circa 1961).

CHAPTER 5

Reaching Back

I was known for reaching back to bring others from North Carolina to DC. With a promise to help my family and friends get on their feet and flourish on their own, I drove my brother, Percy, to DC in 1955 and later went back to get my baby sister, Joyce, in 1956. Percy was a hard sell, while Joyce just needed to know where to put her bags.

It was a no brainer to make an investment in my brother who had done so much for our family when we were struggling. When there was no food in the house, Percy, along with my brother, Preston, would work longer hours at a furniture plant to help out.

When I was 15 years old, I received my driver's license. My father, unknowingly, signed a document that said I was 16 years old. Even though I was underage, Percy still let me drive his car. He took a chance on me and I appreciated it.

One thing I remember most about Percy is his care and consideration. Even when I had a serious accident in his car and totaled it, he was compassionate

My skull was fractured, but I was scared of what Percy Percy would do to me. Instead of berating me, he showed love.

"Forget about the car. Are you hurt?" Percy asked. Percy was more concerned about me than a material object.

When I saw an opportunity for Percy to make more money in DC than he did in Franklinton, I asked him to come up to experience a taste of the good life. Instead of Percy rushing to claim his piece of the pie, he kept giving me reasons why he couldn't move:

1. I don't know my way around DC.
2. I don't have any money.
3. I don't have a place to stay.

His reasons were minor to me. So, I offered Percy my car, space in my home to sleep, and promised to talk management into giving him my job at Emergency Hospital where I worked. Percy finally agreed. I went to get Percy from Franklinton and drove him back to DC with me.

As promised, I gave him my job and my car, and

in three days, God showed me favor and restored my employment with a new job. It was only three blocks from home. I began work as a driver for Standard Tobacco Company.

Percy, worked at Emergency Hospital for several years. It was also the place where he met his wife, Mary. They built a life together and had three children--- Rhonda, Robin, and Warren.

Percy later worked two jobs at the same time. He worked at a printing company delivering packages and moved up the ranks and became a printing press operator for documents that were delivered to Capitol Hill. His second job was with Colonial Parking—he worked with me at night.

After a week of working and taking care of our families, we spent our Friday nights playing cards. If Percy lost or spent all of his money, he would borrow money from me. He would always pay me back, even if he had to borrow it from someone else to do so.

Percy had made a way for himself and his family. Joyce did as well. In fact, she and Percy lived in the same apartment building. Joyce lived upstairs with her husband, Merlin, and Percy lived directly below them.

Joyce worked at a laundry service with my wife, Juanita. Several years later, she was appointed to a very high level position with Chartered Health Plan—the company from which she retired in 2004.

Percy had seemingly built a comfortable life for Mary and the children and made a great salary, but saving money was a challenge for him. Then his light drinking turned heavier. While Percy's drinking increased, he never let his love for his children wane. They were his life.

I was told that one night Percy came home and took his gun out of his pocket. The gun accidentally went off and he shot himself in the head. It was said that one of the children went to Joyce's apartment and knocked on the door and told Joyce their father had been shot. She and Merlin rushed downstairs to Percy's aid.

They called for an ambulance, but it didn't come quickly enough. I am told Merlin carried Percy over his shoulder and down the stairs so he could take him to the hospital in his car. As Merlin carried Percy, Joyce flagged down a police officer. The officer let them ride in the back of the car with Percy lying across their laps and in Merlin's arms. When they arrived at the hospital, they tried to resuscitate Percy, but couldn't.

Joyce called me, and I met them at the hospital. When I arrived, I did not see Mary with them. I was too worried about my brother making it out of this incident alive to find out why. Unfortunately, Percy died in the police car on March 21, 1971; he was 39 years old.

When the police began filing a report, they became suspicious of Joyce and Merlin and thought they had shot Percy because they had blood on their clothes. The police interrogated Merlin and Joyce and threatened to take them to jail. Before making an arrest, the police went back to Percy's apartment to speak with his wife to determine what happened and to fill in the gaps. The police let them go after speaking with Mary.

Tragically, his three children were in the room watching television when the incident happened. After that, Mary and the children moved to a different place because the children began having nightmares. The children were constantly reminded of the night their father died. It was replayed in their minds.

I always had a fondness for Percy's children, much like I did with Evelyn's children. In his absence, I tried to be as much of a male presence in their lives as I was with my own children. They were very much a part of my family, and I never let them forget that as they grew up. They were seeds of Percy. It was my job to help them grow, much like Percy had done for me when I was younger.

CHAPTER 6

Staying Alive. Staying Employed.

While working as a driver for Standard Tobacco Company, I met a life long friend, Eddie Copeland. Eddie had a part time job at a parking lot, Colonial Parking. I needed some extra cash to support my family, so Eddie put in a good word for me. I got the job.

I worked for Colonial Parking on a part-time basis for 12 years. We worked alongside each other at both Standard Tobacco Company and Colonial Parking. We worked out a way that kept both of us employed if the other person was out of work---job sharing at Colonial Parking. We would share the work of a full time job that had a seven-day workweek. Here's how it worked:

Eddie would work three days one week and four days the next week and vice versa. Both of us had a wife and four kids. We told each other if either of us lost our job, the other would give up his days so the other person would have full time hours. Would you believe Eddie's company closed? So I gave Eddie two of my days so he could make up the difference in time. I kept one day of work until Eddie got another job, and then I went back to working three days a week. I worked there for two years before I was promoted to supervisor.

I was never a stranger to hard work or ambition. After befriending James Jones, the station manager at a service station just two blocks from my home, I was given the green light to volunteer my time helping him. In exchange, I learned how to manage and operate a gas station. I would volunteer my time at the service station with Mr. Jones on my days off from Colonial Parking.

My responsibilities increased as our business relationship grew. Mr. Jones told me he would give me one-half ownership of the station. I had to pay him back out of my pay until my 50% was paid. I was 23 years old at the time. By 1958, I had become the manager of the gas station. I left my full-time job and started working for myself. My keen marketing and financial skills helped me to double the station's business in 12 months.

Once I had a taste of self-employment, I moved on to other ventures. One of my regular customers at the gas station was the owner of a dump truck business, Grant. He was successful. We became friends and partners. I was feeling pretty confident one day and expressed my interest in his line of work.

"If I buy a dump truck, will you teach me the business?" I asked him, and he said, "Yes."

Since my credit was good, I worked out a payment plan for Mr. Jones to let me buy his share of the gas station. I paid him until the balance was zero.

I used money from my savings account to begin investing in my dump truck business. I knew I couldn't just go to a dealer and say, "Hey, I want to buy one of your trucks. Here's the money." I had to secure a written contract with a company committed to doing business with me. My first contract was hauling materials for the construction of the second 14th Street Bridge in Washington, D.C. With the appropriate paperwork in hand, I went to a Chevrolet dealership, and the salesman gave me a new, 10-wheel dump truck with a little money down. I drove the dump truck and hired my brother-in-law, my sister Joyce's first husband, Frederick Spivey, to work at the gas station so I could drive the truck full-time.

We had some really high profile contracts, including hauling dirt and rocks on the land where the

Washington Hilton now stands on Florida Avenue in DC. In addition, I had a contract with the District of Columbia for snow removal during the winter. Things were moving along very well for Bradford and Grant. In no time, Grant and I bought another 10-wheel dump truck and grew our company.

The gas station and the dump truck company were merged. As the business flourished, we made more investments in it. We bought two more 10-wheel dump trucks, and with each increasing success, we became "big headed." Our excess money went towards luxury purchases. We bought race cars, boats, and motorcycles. It was the folly of someone who had money to burn and neglected the eventual consequences of the future.

We spent money as if there was no end to it. We were spending beyond our means. Then the bad winters came. There was no work – in the winter, the ground freezes and construction comes to a halt. Because we were careless with our spending, we did not have enough money to support us or the business---not even for 90 days.

When financial troubles hit, my thinking goes into

overdrive and survival mode. So I suggested to my business partner that we scale down and give three dump trucks away and let the new owners assume the payments. We could cut cost and drive the other two dump trucks. He was not sold on the idea.

"I am not going to give away three of our dump trucks. If you are going to give away the three dump trucks and let a stranger assume the payments, let me take that deal. I'll keep making the payments on the trucks," he said.

I gave him the deal and left the company. However, what I didn't know is if I didn't take my name off the company's documents, I would still be responsible for the business and its obligations.

After leaving the dump truck business, I went to work for a grocery store, Giant Foods, as a porter just to provide for my wife and children. However, nine months down the road, I was informed that Grant did not pay the District of Columbia Government taxes or Federal taxes to the Internal Revenue Service (IRS). Consequently, the IRS came after me because I had assets, a house and a job. I obtained a second mortgage on my house and got another job so I could pay the IRS what was owed. This was not a time to fold and run. I had to take responsibility for what seemed to be an impossible task—paying the IRS more than $20,000, plus interest and penalties. My former business partner didn't have any money, and he didn't have a job.

During this time, my wife had stopped working a full-time job because she started a childcare business. It was very difficult carrying the load alone. I was so distraught about my financial situation, especially the amount that I owed to the IRS, I started driving toward the 14th Street Bridge, fully intending to take my life. This was the same bridge that my trucks were used to haul sand and gravel to build. On my way there, it was as if the voice of God spoke to me and said, "You owe them; they don't owe you!"

In essence, the IRS had to wait and worry about me paying them back. I didn't have to stress about waiting on someone to pay me back. At that moment, I changed courses and haven't looked back and didn't allow the "I can't" attitude to set in. I just did what had to be done. It took me eight years to get out of debt. Lesson learned.

My success didn't stop. I kept climbing.
Vice President of Sales and Operations - 1982

CHAPTER 7

Moving up like the Jeffersons

In 1966, I frequented a restaurant next door to the Giant Foods store where I worked. A man named Hank Walker worked for a distributing company that sold Pabst Blue Ribbon beer. Hank and I would eat together sometimes. Hank drove one of the Pabst trucks. This was almost unheard of during this time. Hank was black and was likely the first black driver in Washington, D.C. Hank had only been in the position two weeks. One day, Hank asked me to work with him on the truck. I was an assistant grocery manager. I couldn't see myself working on a delivery truck. However, I took a chance on changing jobs and was hired. I would follow in his footsteps and become the second black driver in the city.

Hank had just finished his training, so he didn't have enough experience to train me. Because I was black, the white drivers wouldn't train me. However, Jimmy, an Asian American, took the time to show me the ropes. I hung on to his every word and action. I wanted to be proficient and efficient at my job.

I earned more money in one week than I earned in two weeks at Giant Foods. Hank and I decided we were going to break all records for driver sales. Hank and I were selling Pabst Blue Ribbon in a 68% black city---a beer blacks didn't normally drink at the time. We sold more Pabst beer in the black areas than the company had ever sold. All of the store owners and warehouse managers started calling us brothers. We kept that title for the duration of our friendship.

During the time Hank and I were selling Pabst, Schlitz was the best selling beer. All of the drivers wanted to sell Schlitz. One day while I was on my route, I heard many of the store owners were talking about my sales record. It was reported to me that the owner of a Schlitz distributor, Morris Bisker, was asking about me.

"Who is this guy I have been hearing so much about? I want him to work for our company." Mr. Bisker asked around. Mr. Bisker sent Wesley Jiles to approach me. He asked me to come by his office to meet Mr. Bisker. Mr. Bisker offered me a job in 1969.

I was hired on the same day as a white driver. Usually, all new employees work on the keg truck and work their way up to the driver salesman position. I got the route salesman job because I had prior sales training from Pabst, and he was put on the keg truck. He was very upset; he felt entitled because he was white.

After serving a year as a route salesman, I was promoted to street salesman. I stayed in that position for 18 months. As I moved up through the company's ranks and became a sales supervisor, I had an employee who would not do anything I asked him to do. He was the same employee who was hired the same day I was hired. He was intentionally insubordinate. This happened consistently month after month. I got fed up and said enough is enough. I fired him.

The guy went to the union and complained. I had to rehire him because I didn't have my performance documentation in order. The union informed me he had to perform the work I requested of him. When he came back, he worked for a short period before complaining to Morris Bisker.

"I can't work for a black man," he told Mr. Bisker.

"Well, I'll accept your resignation because Jesse is managing the company. That includes drivers, warehouse, and office staff," Mr. Bisker told him.

In essence, Mr. Bisker made things clear: the guy had no place in the company if he could not work for me. He decided to quit. He would rather sacrifice a job paying $40,000 to $45,000 a year in the 1970s and work for less because he didn't want to work for a black man.

At Schlitz, I was given increasingly more responsible positions. I was a top sales supervisor. My sales were up 125% each month. Yes, it's possible. I won the sales supervisor of the month 11 out of 12 months. I still have the plaques as a reminder that I, a little boy from Franklinton, North Carolina, had really beaten the odds despite many obstacles.

For a year or two, things were going well. Then a tragedy happened. The warehouse manager had a heart attack and died in my arms before help arrived. After that, 50% of the company was sold to another person, a black man, Vernon Coleman. The company was in the red. Mr. Coleman hired four different sales managers who were not able to turn the company around. I had to train all of them. After Mr. Coleman started the process of hiring the fifth sales manager, I told both owners I was tired of training managers and asked them to give me the opportunity to perform the job. Mr. Coleman said, "If you take the job and don't make it, I will have to fire you." I took the challenge.

Mr. Coleman told me I was going to have trouble with one of the high level supervisors because he didn't believe I deserved the appointment. I suggested that both of us be given the same pay and title. Both of us were promoted to Assistant Vice President. That change helped some. However, I did not have any power. I could not get the job done. I asked for the authority to hire and terminate staff. In order to accommodate this new authority, the owners changed their titles – one to Chairman of the Board and the other to Managing Partner. The Assistant Vice President and I were moved to Vice President and General Manager to run the entire company.

The day I was promoted to Assistant Vice President and General Manager was bittersweet. I was so happy about my new accomplishment. Juanita and I had been married for 15 years at this time. I went home and told her about the promotion and asked if she would prepare a special dinner for me. Her response shocked me.

"No, because you are a fool to take that job. I will not rejoice in your failure. I have been through this with you with the dump trucks," she said.

I tucked my head in disappointment and went to McDonalds for dinner and sat by myself to think long and hard about the job I had just accepted. I prayed about it. It was as if God spoke to me and said, "Go and I will go with you." I know, to this day, God has continued to stay with me.

I told my wife I was going to take the job. From that day forward, my wife hated my job.

Around this time, my daughter, my second child, was nineteen and pregnant with my first grandchild. I went crazy; I was very angry with her. I wanted to mangle the boy who got her pregnant, and I wanted to put my child out of my house. After a few days, I came to my senses and let the boy live and my daughter stay in the house.

Vashawn, my granddaughter, was born nine months later. I instantly fell in love with her. Vashawn would become a great highlight in my life. She became the grandchild whose bright spirit and love was unconditional and pure, no matter where I lived. Her success would become my success.

After being promoted to Vice President and General Manager, I had to work nights and travel extensively. I tried to get Juanita to travel with me; she wouldn't. She said she was a church member, and I sold beer—something the church did not approve of. She did not want to be a part of selling beer.

I had to attend a lot of formal balls by myself because she would not go with me. As a result of my having to attend company and other functions by myself and realizing my wife's attention was also elsewhere, I started dating a school teacher. Initially, we were not dating. At my request, she agreed to help me with my company paper work because I did not want the company to know I did not have a college degree. The lady and I became close friends. This relationship lasted for a long time, and then it ended. This is something I am not proud of. In 1985, my wife and I separated.

Schlitz experienced another tragedy while I was Vice President and General Manager. Another ware-house manager was opening the warehouse at 5 a.m. He was mugged and murdered during the robbery. It was reported his body was put in the trunk of his car and was taken to Rock Creek Park in Washington, D.C. His remains were reported to have been dumped in a nearby body of water. It was also reported by the police that while an unknown lady was driving his car, blood dripped from the trunk. The police stopped the car. The woman was so scared she told the police what happened.

I was called at home to identify the body. It was very difficult to keep the team focused that day.

In the face of tragedy, I was still able to climb the ladder of success, but it did not come without hard work. I had a lot of proving to do. My appointment to the position of Vice President and General Manager came at a time when Schlitz's sales plummeted because of a batch of substandard beer. It was my time to show I could be successful or become a failure for trying to do the impossible. I chose to do the former.

Since I was in a struggle to keep my job, change had to be made.

"I need to make some cuts," I told the managers. In order for Schlitz to come out on top, each person had to work harder. I proposed to give each remaining employee an 8% to 10% raise with the money I would save from the layoffs. The owners approved my request. So, on a Friday, we terminated 13 out of 73 people; gave 30 people in sales a 10% raise and the other 30 an 8% raise. That day became known as Black Friday at Schlitz.

We worked around the clock during the day, at night, and on weekends. The company stopped its downslide and started to turn around. My job retention prospects looked better. I made changes to the process used by the route salespersons to sell beer. At first all of the beer was on one truck. I took Bull and Old Milwaukee off the main trucks and put them on four Schlitz Malt Liquor Bull trucks. We went to Schlitz and asked them for a car to give away as a Bull promotion with WHUR 96.3 FM, a local station on Howard University's campus in DC. The Bull sales went through the roof! This sales trend went on for five years. I was a total success in the eyes of the Schlitz's owners and my immediate manager.

The company also had Old English Malt Liquor. I went to Pabst and told them about the success Bull had with the car give-away. They gave me an SUV to give away in partnership with another local radio station owned by Cathy Hughes. It was an AM radio station.

Beer companies would not advertise on Hughes' station because the Arbitron ratings were low. So I went to Cathy and told her I would give her an opportunity to promote the car give-away. That advertising helped to put her AM station on the map. Other beer companies would now look at her station because the advertising rates were low. Today, Cathy and her son, Alfred Liggins, own more than 50 radio stations and a TV station (TV One). I used my success to promote success throughout my community.

Even when I retired in 1998, I made it my business to keep promoting those who had dreams and wanted to truly taste the fruit of their labor. While my hard work afforded me the opportunity to retire at age 62, build my dream home in Florida, and to be debt free, I couldn't stand by and watch others struggle without giving them a formula that works.

In my retirement, I continue to teach young adults to refuse to say, "I can't" in the face of their struggles. Under "the plan" I share, success takes time to build. Even while they work their way to the top, they will have to face obstacles. Knowing what to do to get through those obstacles determines how long they stay in the midst of their storms.

I still live by the motto: *If you don't have a plan, you plan to fail.* Saying "I can" comes with a plan. Those who believe they can't or won't try never intend to look beyond their circumstances. Which side will you choose?

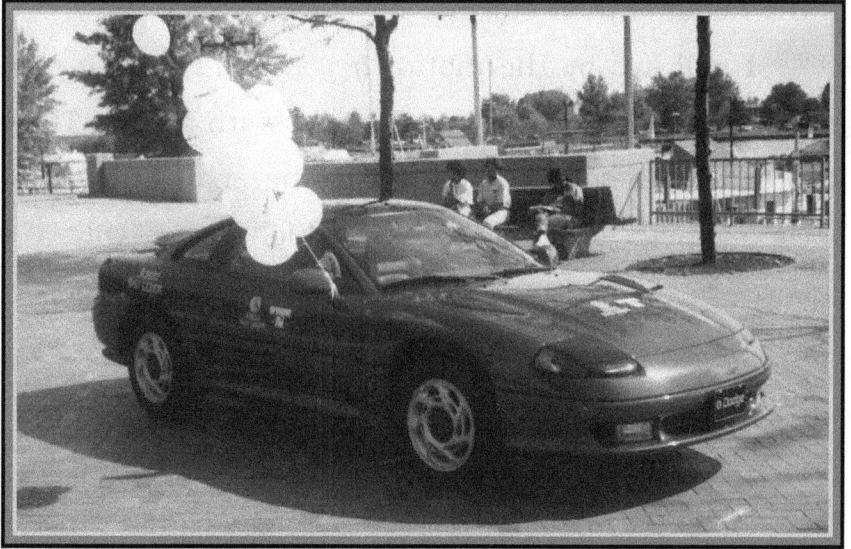

A Schlitz and WHUR-FM Promotion
A lucky person won this car.

CHAPTER 8

Making An Impact

Mario

While I was working at Schlitz, I interviewed a guy for a mechanic position to work on the company trucks. His name is Mario. When I first met Mario, I smiled and said to him, "The tires on these trucks are as tall as you are." Mario was quick to respond, and assured me tall tires were no problem for him.

"I've worked on truck tires before," he said with confidence.

I hired Mario, and he proved to be the best man for the job. He did excellent work. Since he was such a good worker, I wanted to help him grow in his career. I allowed him to keep the garage open after hours so he could work on some of the employees' cars at a reasonably rate. Planting that seed was a stepping stone toward helping Mario open an auto repair service independent of his job. I still send business his way, even though I'm 900 miles away.

Brace yourselves for Brenda.

Schlitz Malt Liquor Bull was one of the highest volume sellers of the malts and beers after the car give away. Each route salesman carried about 15 different brands of beer on a truck. Since Bull was in demand, I requested that Bull be placed on its own truck. My request was approved.

When I changed the trucks from Schlitz to Bull, I hired two telephone sales ladies. One of those individuals was Brenda Bracy.

Prior to coming to Schlitz in DC, she worked in telephone sales in Maryland at another Schlitz branch. She had asked her supervisor (her brother-in-law) if he would promote her to street sales. He denied her request. She contacted me and asked if she could be moved to our distribution center in Washington, D.C. I looked at her sales record before saying yes. It was impeccable.

"You need to be on our street sales team," I said to her. Brenda didn't cringe at the challenge. So I just gave her one piece of advice for her to continue her success.

"You will have to carry your own load to show people you can do as well as any of the men on the team," I continued. Brenda hit the ground running, and she kept tripling her telephone sales.

When I promoted her to street sales, once again, Brenda broke records and set trends. She out sold all of my male salesmen, and she continued to excel until my retirement in 1998.

The Schlitz distributorship acquired a Budweiser distributorship a few years prior to my retirement. Before leaving the beer industry, I asked Budweiser to promote Brenda to my position. They, instead, promoted her to a team leader position at a salary that was lower than what I had earned. She accepted the position, but a few years later, Brenda moved on to a Miller distributorship as a manager.

While Brenda was able to get the experience of managing a team, she realized she liked sales a bit more. There's something about the perks that come along with the adventures in sales.

Faithful Charlie Less

Charlie Less was one of the hardest working employees I have ever had the pleasure of supervising. When I came to American Sales, the Schlitz distributor, he was a truck driver like me. Later, I was promoted to Vice President and General Manager. One day, when I was riding with him on his route, he expressed an interest in being a supervisor. I recognized that he had the temperament and skills needed to lead people. Without hesitation I promoted him to the next available sales supervisor position.

You could always depend on Charlie to do what you asked of him with integrity and in the manner that you wanted it done. One year, I had to travel to Germany to represent the company at a conference. I asked Charlie to fill in for me during my absence. He ran the company smoothly.

Charlie was a very responsible employee. So, when he asked me if his sons could work at the company during the summer, my immediate response was, "Yes." I figured that the apple wouldn't fall too far from the tree. His sons worked for the company during the summer months. One of his sons still works in the beer business.

Charlie later wanted a change from his sales supervisor position. I reassigned Charlie to serve as the warehouse supervisor – the position from which he retired. I am forever grateful to Charlie for his efforts.

CHAPTER 9

Entrepreneurship

I am a very hardworking and ambitious person who believes in helping others to be the best they can be. I started several companies while in DC. I started a vending company with two pinball machines. When PacMan and Galaxy came out, the machines became really profitable. I went from two pinball machines to 200 pinball machines, juke boxes, pool tables, and other machines, including pay phones. In 1994, I, along with a partner named Jimmy---not the guy who trained me at Pabst, started a house cleaning business—East Coast Enterprise. I gave Jimmy 49% just to run the company, and I owned 51%. My partner and I worked together for four years.

In 1998, I gave Jimmy my 51% of the partnership. I also sold my vending company to my sister, Joyce, Merlin, and their son, Andre', for only 40% of its net worth because Joyce had promised she would give Andre' 33% of the company after it was paid for. I then sold Merlin and Joyce my house for $50,000 less than what it was worth. In exchange, I asked Joyce and

Merlin to sell their house to Andre' and give him $25,000 off the market value of their house so he could have a leg up on his future. I had promised Andre' if he would work with me with the vending, I would make sure he was taken care of when I retired. I kept my promise, and Andre has created his own legacy of entrepreneurship following "the plan".

CHAPTER 10

Family Ties

I married Juanita at the age of 18, and I had my first child at 19, Sherrard---three others followed: Sherran, Nikeith, and TiJuan. I purchased my first home at the age of 22. This was something my father never had a chance to do. Looking back at all the opportunities I had with a limited education, I'm able to see my children excel in various areas of their lives as well.

All of our children went to public schools. Their high school, Eastern High School, had a high incidence of drug use. In spite of that, I did not remove them from Eastern. I talked with them about making positive decisions. I helped each one of them to get a car at age 16 provided they stay drug free. No one wanted to give up their car for drugs.

Sherrard went to Talladega College in Alabama. He graduated and started working for a local government agency in DC; he is still employed with them.

Prior to attending college, Sherrard was an

inspiration and a positive influence to many of the younger children in the community. He started and coached a football team in order to keep children off the streets. Sherrard, like me, was a self-starter and an entrepreneur. He would sell different products in order to make money for himself prior to attending and while he attended college. So it looks like the apple didn't fall too far from the tree.

Sherran, my daughter and second child, went to college as well, but didn't finish. Instead, she secured a job working for Metro, DC's public transportation system. She is still working for them. She moved up the ladder pretty quickly. She began as a bus driver and is now in a supervisory position with the company.

Sherran seems to fit the norm of girls maturing faster than boys. She was a very independent person; she moved out on her own at an earlier age than all of my boys. She, like me, is also an entrepreneur. Even though she is a supervisor and makes a great salary, she still sells ladies purses and other accessories.

Nikeith, or Nicky as we call him, is my third child. He went to college; he didn't finish either. As a result, I hired him to work for me at Schlitz, and I also gave him a part-time job working for my vending and video game company. I first sent him to school to learn how to repair pinball machines.

Nicky has always been a happy-go-lucky person. I say the following with a loving heart: Nicky and money don't stay together very long – just as it didn't with my brother, Percy. In Nicky's defense, he has a big heart; he will give you the shirt off his back. Whatever you ask of him, it's done without a second thought. Nicky has always been there for me whenever I needed him. When I was alone in Orlando, Florida, he moved to be near me in the event I became ill; I really appreciate it, and will never forget it.

TiJuan, my youngest, went to college as well and didn't finish, initially. He decided to work for the U.S. Postal Service. He later decided to go back to college and earned a degree.

TiJuan is very talented. He loves music and excels in the profession as a performer and as a leader. He is a wonderful choir director at a local church in Washington, D.C. TiJuan also worked with me early on with the vending and video game company. He would run vending routes for me so I wouldn't have to do them by myself – but he also needed and wanted to make some spare change to keep himself clothed with the latest fashions.

I taught my children the value of being able to take care of themselves.

"If you don't have a job working for someone else, you should know how to make a living on your own," I told them.

Each of my children had a part in helping me sell ladies and men's clothing and accessories. Teaching my children how to be self-sufficient is the greatest gift I could have given them. It was my hope that my life's journey would serve as an inspiration to my children.

Unfortunately, Juanita and I divorced before I could fully mentor my children as adults. Divorce is never pleasant, but it is a painful part of life when a husband and wife just can't find common ground. Lives are impacted emotionally as well as financially.

After the divorce, I was nearly broke. I went right back to the same McDonald's where I celebrated the success of my promotion, alone. I had only $20,000 in my savings account, and I owed $120,000 on my house and car. My goal was to retire at age 62; so I knew I had to get on the fast track. I said I would be out debt in five years because I had no one to take care of but me. I had a significant financial hurdle to overcome for at least 8 to 9 years following the divorce. I had no money for dates or parties. This was a time of complete discipline, tenacity, and a lot of loneliness. My youngest child, TiJuan, lived with me for one year following the divorce.

When it looked like I was going to lose everything (after nearly depleting all of my assets), including my house, TiJuan, seemingly, felt more comfortable living with his mother. His mother's house was already paid for, and it was unlikely she would be losing her home.

Since I came back from a major disaster after giving away the dump trucks and closing my service station business in 1964, I was able to rebound again. On the outside, some may have thought I couldn't bounce back, but I believed in myself enough to try because I had weathered financial troubles in the past.

I said to myself, "I can come back from this." So, I put a plan in place. With debt at $120,000 and $30,000 in interest, I paid $2,500 per month and paid off my house and car in five years. The plan worked like clockwork, but I could not save any money during those five years. Yet, I knew I had only 17 years following those five years to save money for my retirement; so I stayed on the fast track. I started saving $3,000 each month for the next 17 years. To supplement my income, I sold two rental properties and my vending machine company – taking back notes on each one.

When I was able to save money, the economy worked in my favor. At that time the interest rate was 10% on the dollar. I was able to retire on time as planned at age 62. In spite of all of these trying circumstances, I did not turn to illegal activities – I did not write illegal numbers, sell or take drugs, or become an alcoholic.

I later married my second wife, Michelle Coleman, on June 6, 1993. We retired to Florida and rented the house Michelle owned. Trying to be a landlord 900 plus miles away was very difficult and very costly. Consequently, Michelle and I decided to sell Merlin and Joyce 33% and André 33% of Michelle's house for only $13,000 each; we took back a note on the house until the loan was paid. This was done in exchange for their management of the house. When things became almost unmanageable with the tenant, we agreed to sell the house. Each of us received about $34,000 each. Following this experience, Andre' understood how owning real estate could be profitable. He continues to invest in real estate today.

While I was making moves to recover my losses, I still missed my children terribly. Before remarrying, I stayed single for 8 years. Sherrard and Sherran did not speak to me for at least two years. Since the divorce, there was never a time when I had all my children gathered together at the same time. After I had worked so hard to keep my family together, this hurt me very badly. I was a lone number two pencil, but somehow had the strength of five like my Great Grandma Millie Ann showed me.

My children would have cookouts and Christmas parties and would not invite me. When I had cookouts, I invited everyone. However, they did not come. I was very lonely because I had spent most of my time with Juanita's family. That is what most men do—spend most of their time with their wife's family.

I was really glad Joyce had moved to D.C. with

me. We were fortunate enough to find our brothers Mack and Arthur in New Jersey with the assistance of an aunt who still lived in Franklinton. We invited them to a family reunion at my house in Washington, D.C. in 1985. We have not lost touch since then. I was rebuilding my family. When I later remarried to a caring woman named Michelle Coleman, I invited all of my children to the wedding. The only ones who attended were Nicky, TiJuan and my granddaughter, Vashawn. When I celebrated my 60th birthday, only Nikeith and Sherran came. When I had my retirement party, only Nicky came.

When I was preparing to move to Florida from DC, I didn't rely on a moving company. I planned the trip and moved on my own. I asked all of my sons to help me pack the truck. Only one of my sons came over to help me; that was Nicky. He helped drive the truck to Florida. My two nephews, Dexter Montague and Andre' Strain, helped me move. Dexter caught the train from Franklinton to Washington, D.C. A cousin, Murad Nuriddin, rented a car and drove from Newport News, VA to DC to help with the move as well. Hank Walker took off from work for four days to help bring the truck and all of the cars I owned to Florida. The move was a task, but it was successful.

When my sister, Evelyn, passed away, my daughter Sherran and her youngest daughter, Juanita attended the funeral. I was extremely close to my sister and this was a time I needed the support of my family; but only one of my children came.

After moving to Orlando, I purchased a motor-cycle and joined an all white motorcycle club. I became the first black admitted to the U.S. Military Veterans Motorcycle Club. My neighbor, *Juice,* introduced me to the club, and Michelle and I became the newsletter editors. I had a new support system. I rode with them until Michelle got sick in 2003; she was diagnosed with cancer.

In 2000, I was diagnosed with colon cancer. I had to have a major operation. I asked my children to come to Florida, just in case I did not survive the surgery. No one came to visit me during this time but my sister, Joyce, Merlin, and their son Andre'. Merlin was ill and could not walk very well. He had one good leg, but he came to be by my side.

71

In 2007, the cancer came back again. I asked my children to come to Florida to ensure that all my personal documents were in order and to ensure their interest was protected. Nicky had already moved to Florida to help me, and I appreciated that. He was at the hospital during my surgery. None of my other children came. TiJuan was in Florida on the day before my surgery. I asked him if he would stay one extra day. He said he couldn't; he went back to DC. The next week he went out of town again on another trip.

Would you believe in 2009, the cancer came back? The doctor told me because I had two colon cancer operations this would be very serious. Again, I asked my children to visit to make sure everything was in order. It seemed not one of my children even cared enough to come. Only Joyce, Andre', Mart and Gwen (his wife) came. Yolonda, Michelle's daughter, came to visit me the week prior to the surgery to cheer me up. Everything turned out fine.

Since I've been living in Florida, my nieces, Robin and Rhonda, and their children would come to Florida to visit me every summer. After their father, Percy, died, I tried to be a father figure for them. They seem to appreciate it. Whenever I am in the Washington, D.C. or the Richmond, VA areas, they make sure they come to visit me – wherever I am. Vashawn has been the only grandchild who has come to visit me without my asking her to do so. She just makes the plan to come, and I welcome her with open arms.

My nieces and nephews seem to demonstrate the love and care I expect from my children. Nikeith, however, has always been there for me whenever I needed him and whenever I asked him for assistance.

I married my current wife, Marie, on February 15, 2008. Marie, and I celebrated a combined family reunion (Bradfords and McNears) on Christmas Day 2009. We started the planning process almost a year earlier and sent invitations to everyone in my family and my wife's family. I spoke to each one of my children individually to invite them. Because I was advancing in age---I was 73 at the time---I asked them to spend just one Christmas with me as adults. The only one of my biological children who came was Nikeith. The others stayed in DC and attended another event they planned long after I had sent them an invitation to attend the reunion.

My nieces and nephews came: Krista (and her husband, Claudius), Sean, Andre' (and his wife Latoya), Fred (we call him Lil' Fred), Robin, Rhonda, and their daughters Dominique, and Chya. My step children, Yolonda (and her husband Sir Dreck and his mother, Justine) and Maxwell (Marie's son and my godson) also came. This was a very important event for me. It was at the Christmas reunion I realized God had put other people in my life to fill the void left by the emptiness I felt from not having my children's love. For this, I am grateful.

CHAPTER 11

Swimming with the Dolphins

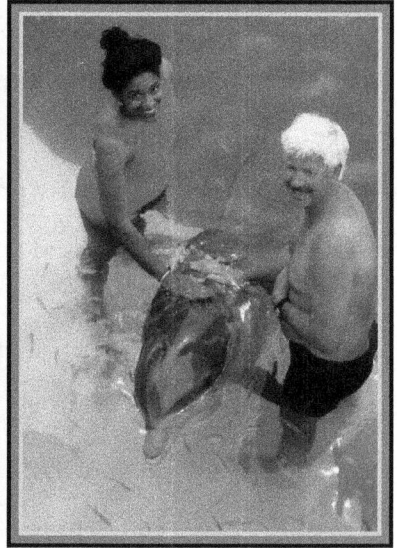

Michelle D. Bradford – my second wife
August 11, 1961 – March 30, 2005

I was young when I first got married and had never really enjoyed the "single life". Now I was enjoying my new life a little too much; it was fun to be dating again.

While I was dating, I met a much younger lady, Michelle Coleman. She was 25 years younger than me. When I was promoted to Vice President of Schlitz and Imports, the company meetings were held at various places. It was during this time I married Michelle Coleman.

Michelle already had a child, Yolonda. She was a good child. She always had good study habits and kept good grades. We sent her to Hampton University where she continued to stay on the honor roll.

Michelle and I traveled when the company scheduled me on business trips. I went to places I never could have imagined I would be able to go because of my background and lack of a college education. That is why I encourage anyone, regardless of their station in life, to never give up or say "I can't" and pursue their dreams regardless of the number of "no" answers they get during their lifetime.

After Yolonda finished college, Michelle and I

moved to Florida. Yolonda did not want to move. For Yolonda not to be my biological child, she displayed the same kind of independence I had when I was her age.

We told Yolonda that as an adult she could make adult decisions as long as she understood the rewards and consequences. So, she remained in DC.

Michelle and I both retired in 1998 and bought our dream home in Orlando, Florida. Yolonda proved to be her own success story. Along the way, she had scrapes and bruises, but she always knew how to recover her losses and modify her plans to get back on track.

Michelle and I were married for 12 years. She died from cancer on March 30, 2005. During her final days as she lay dying, she called Yolonda and me to her bedside and said she wanted me to go on with my life after her death. She told me to find someone who was going to care for me and who would take care of me. She was concerned about me, even though she was in pain and dying.

When Michelle died, only Sherrard and his wife and daughter, Jeanette and JaNece, came to the funeral.

It was very difficult to watch someone die for two years. Michelle told me if she passed first, she wanted to be cremated and she wanted her ashes spread in the sea in Mexico with the dolphins. I kept that promise, even though some of her family members were against the cremation.

Yolonda, Mike (Michelle's brother), his wife, Barbara, and I took a cruise to Mexico on May 19, 2005. At midnight, the captain of the ship slowed the vessel and granted us permission to spread her ashes in international waters, with the dolphins, as she wished.

I was glad I had the resources to grant her last wish.

CHAPTER 12
My 1st Corinthians 13:4-7 Wife: Marie Bradford

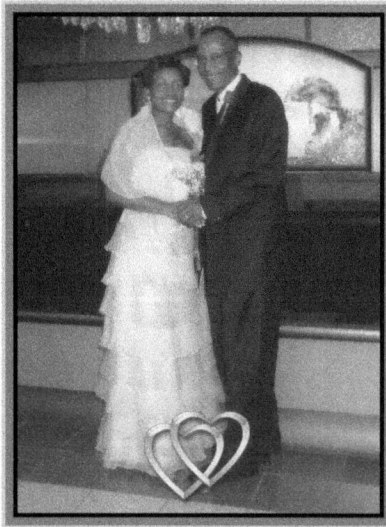

I stayed single for three years after Michelle passed. I met my current wife, Marie, in 1986. She was having similar relationship challenges. We became close friends. She helped me with my company's administrative work. She lived about five blocks from my office. So, I would go to her house to get assistance. We spent a lot of time together.

By the time things progressed, we were both divorced. We began to date. She asked me if I would be her son's Godfather. I accepted. Marie and I dated for several years. My lack of a single life during my younger years had an impact on my desire to be monogamous. So I changed things up a bit and dated others, including Michelle – my second wife. Marie left the relationship. However, we remained friends, and I continued to play a part in her son's life as his godfather.

In February 2006, Marie visited me to determine whether or not we wanted to consider rekindling our relationship. We talked extensively about what we wanted in a relationship. We finally made the decision to get back together – after I was given the third degree! Marie moved to Florida in June 2006. She had real estate in DC. She sold her condo and then later sold her house. She left an eleven-year relationship and friends she had made over a 30-year plus period – a very difficult decision, but she made it.

I continue to ignore the "no" answers I get and negative comments as I age. Friends told me it was too early for me to get married so soon after my second wife had passed. However, I do not like being alone. I needed someone in my life I trusted and who I felt would be there for me in the good as well as the rough times. I needed someone who believed I would also be there for them. I got married to my best friend, Mayola Marie Bradford, on February 15, 2008. We are very happy with our life together.

Jesse L. Bradford

A letter to other little boys and girls

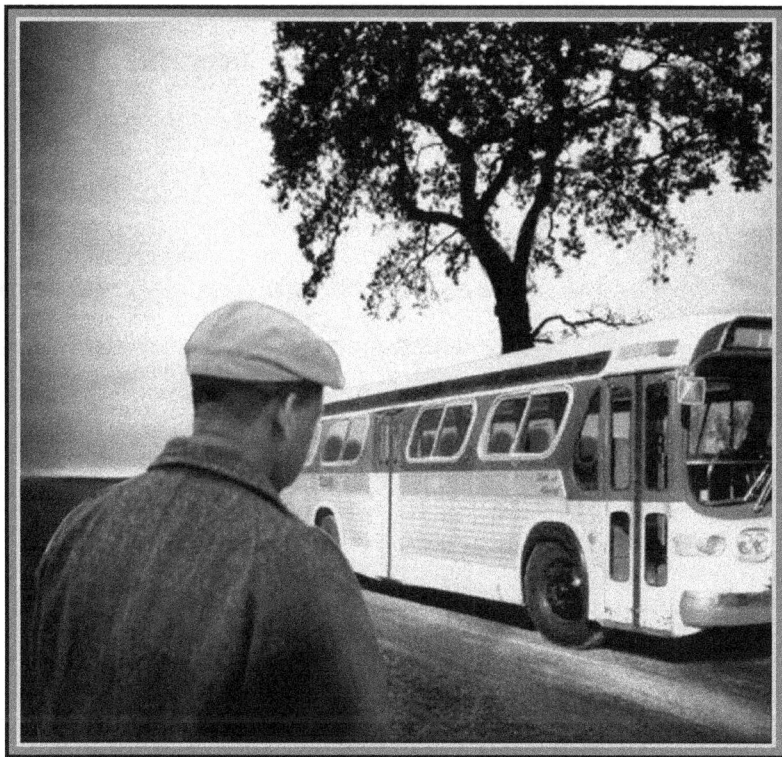

I know it's tough growing up in a world where the glitz and glamour shown on television outweighs the integrity of working your way up. Overnight success stories and local drug dealers make their lifestyle look fun and easy, but hard work trumps fast money anytime.

When you experience the journey toward your dreams, you'll be more willing to protect your future and maintain the fruits of your labor once you get there. You'll also become a teacher to those who want to be a success story. Being a positive influence gives you greater rewards in the future, but remember you always have to have both short term and long term plans.

My consistent hard work yielded various creature comforts. By listing the material items I earned, I am not boasting; I'm just illustrating what you can attain in spite of the "no" answers you may receive throughout your life.

I owned my first house at the age of 22. This was something my father never had a chance to do. I've owned five others since my first purchase, two of which I was able to rent and earn an income from without occupying them. Because of careful planning, I was able to pay cash for my dream home and live comfortably knowing I own it with no payments.

Securing a job with perks and travel benefits afforded me the opportunity to visit places beyond my wildest imagination on someone else's dime. Over time, I've traveled throughout the U.S. as well as outside of the U.S. in places like Germany and France. I either traveled for business, because I won trips due to my outstanding sales record or for pleasure because I had the resources to take a vacation.

Pack your bags as you take a trip with me.

DATE OF TRAVEL	DESTINATION
June 1979	Germany (business)
July 1979	France (business)
May 1986	Jamaica (business)
February 1987	Seven Springs, PA (business)

March 1987	Caribbean & Mexico (business cruise)
May 1987	Miami, Florida (business)
June 1988	Orlando, Florida (business)
August 1989	Ireland (business)
March 1990	Cancun, Mexico (cruise)
June 1990	Hawaii (business)
October 1990	Bermuda (leisure)
February 1991	Atlantic City, NJ (leisure)
June 1991	Nassau, Bahamas (business)
November 1991	Cancun, Mexico (business)

August 1992	Aruba (business cruise)
November 1992	Puerto Vallarta, Mexico (business cruise)
June 1993	Hawaii (honeymoon)
December 1993	Orlando, Florida (incentive)
July 1994	Acapulco, Mexico (business)
September 1994	Freeport, Bahamas (business cruise)
June 1995	Orlando, Florida (business)
June 1996	Cancun, Mexico (business incentive prize cruise)
October 1996	Orlando, Florida (business)
March 1997	Atlanta, GA (business)

June 1997	Freeport, Bahamas (incentive cruise)
March 1998	Orlando, Florida (leisure)
June 1998	San Francisco, CA (business)
August 1998	Nassau, Bahamas (incentive)
November 1998	Orlando, Florida (leisure)
July 2007	Italy, Turkey, Greece (cruise)
February 2008	Bahamas (honeymoon)
February 2009	Mexico (wedding anniversary)
October 2009	Ocho Rios

While real estate and travel are very important, having reliable transportation is just as important. I took care of everything I owned. Like many little boys, I loved cars. So when I grew up, I made sure my budget included the purchase of quality cars. I guess you can say I was a motor vehicle collector. Again, with a plan, you can begin a collection of your own for whatever it is you love.

YEAR	MAKE	MODEL	COLOR
1946	Buick (convertible)		Black
1949	Ford (sedan)		Green and Beige
1956	Ford (sedan)		Red and Black
1959	Pontiac (convertible)	Bonneville	Orange and Black
1962	Pontiac (convertible)	Bonneville	White
1964	Pontiac (convertible)	Bonneville	White and Black
1964	Ford (coupe)	Mustang	Yellow and Black
1966	Pontiac (convertible)	Bonneville	White and Black
1970	Cadillac (convertible)	Deville	Gold and Black
1974	Cadillac (convertible)	Eldorado	Brown
1976	Cadillac (convertible)	Eldorado	Beige and Brown
1978	Chevy (van)		Brown and Beige

COMPANY CARS I DROVE OVER A 10 YEAR SPAN.

MAKE	MODEL	COLOR
Plymouth (sedan)	1979	Black
Ford	T-Bird- 1981	Gold and White
Pontiac (sedan)	Bonneville- 1983	Black and Gold
Chrysler (sedan)	Suburban- 1985	Grey and Black

CARS I BOUGHT ON MY OWN

YEAR	MAKE	MODEL	COLOR
1986	Mercedes Benz (sedan)	420 SEL	Beige
1994	BMW (convertible)	325	Black
1998	Mercedes Benz (sedan)	E320	Silver
1999	Chevrolet (truck)	S10	Burgundy
2002	Jeep (SUV)	Cherokee 4.7	Red
2006	BMW (sedan)	750li	Black
2006	BMW (convertible)	Z4 Roadster	Blue and Black
2010	Cadillac (SUV)	Crossover	Red

Jesse L. Bradford

MOTORCYCLES

350 HONDA

750 HONDA

1000 GOLDWING

1100 HONDA SPORTS

1500 KAWASAKI

You can have what you want as long as you're willing to get the desires of your heart the right way.

When it is all said and done, you want to be proud of the things you have acquired and know you've earned them the right way. Fast money, fast cars, and everything else in the fast lane are sure to end as fast as you got it.

Take lessons from my journey and learn. Understand I have made mistakes along the way in business as well as in my personal endeavors. My desire to better myself and to bring others along with me on the road to success kept me getting up every time I fell. Your life is no different. You just have to see beyond your circumstances and make up your mind to be your own success. Thank you for taking this journey with me.

RECOLLECTIONS ABOUT OUR UNCLE
With Love, Percy's Jewels
Robin, Rhonda, and Warren

I always thought of Uncle Jesse as my cool, hip uncle. As far back as I can remember *he had it goin' on;* he was always well dressed and driving a shiny new car. Uncle Jesse has a fun spirit that is infectious and ageless, which is why I have always enjoyed being around him.

As a child, I liked spending time with him and his family for weekend sleepovers and accompanying them on outings, including church services. My sister and I would also go with him and the family to his company picnics. We enjoyed the good and plentiful food, as well as the games and sports. We especially liked the pony rides. At times, my parents would attend these outings. But if they didn't attend, he still included his two nieces, Robin and Rhonda.

Today, as a parent myself, I have enjoyed watching my daughter get to know her Uncle Jesse or as he prefers "JB" since his looks are youthful and we *grown-ups* would age him. ☺

Once JB retired and moved from the Washington,

91

D.C. area to live in his *dream* home in Orlando, Florida, we continued to have great visits with him. My sister and I traveled to Florida each May at the end of the school year so my daughter, Dominique, and her daughter, Chya, could spend time with JB and his wife. We continued this happy ritual for several years. We would spend a week at his house, which is so conveniently close to the Disney and Universal theme parks and so many other attractions there. One favorite place of our daughters is called Fun Spot. JB suggested it because he figured the girls would really enjoy the race track and other activities there. He was so right!

On two occasions our brother, Warren, joined us on the road trip, including the year his son, Christopher, came along. Those road trips will always be some of our favorite travel memories. It was a good time for my siblings and me to bond, as well as enjoy time with the brother of our dad, Percy, who passed away many, many years ago. We always have a great time with our Uncle Jesse, who is forever the consummate host; ready with entertaining places and or new restaurants for us to try out.

NEPHEW MART'S MEMORIES

The earliest memory of Jesse I can recall is his visit with my mother in Franklinton, N.C. in a brand new convertible Pontiac Bonneville (c 1960). It must have made a huge impression because I was no more than four years old at the time. What I remember most about that day is Jesse and my mother, Evelyn, tried to get me to pose on the hood of the car, but it was so hot on that hood I made a terrible racket. I think they managed to get the photo done, but I will never forget the heat on that hood.

All of my earliest memories of Jesse were based on the cars he drove. I was so impressed because I did not know any black people who drove brand new cars. That is probably when I decided I wanted to emulate his success. I always looked forward to his coming to Franklinton, North Carolina to see what he was driving.

As time went on, I began to realize the cars JB drove were the result of hard work on his part. I remember going to visit him in DC and watching him come home from one job, take a nap in the recliner, and head out to another.

Even though I was just a grade school student at the time, I sensed this was the type of work ethic that was necessary to achieve things in life. Even though, I later learned his first house was essentially a small townhouse, I recall being very impressed by it as a child. Once again, growing up rural, poor Franklinton, I did not know any black folks with a two story house with a basement.

I also fondly recall visiting JB at his office with my mother and my brother, Dexter. He was in charge of running the entire operation, and I was in awe. The proud look on my mother's face spoke volumes.

I thought if I wanted to instill that same feeling in my mom, I would have to achieve the same accomplishments as her little brother. That was one of the turning points for me. I saw, for the first time, a black man with humble beginnings could become special if he had the courage to make the effort. That was inspirational.

As I grew older and spent time around JB during the summers, I realized he was a very resourceful person. Not only did he work two jobs, he also tapped into the video game craze during the 1980s and made substantial sums of money by owning vending machines. I went out with him on collection day and watched him rake in the most quarters I had ever seen in my life. That was a real revelation for me.

One thing I admire Jesse for is his willingness to serve as a mentor for those who wish to learn from his experiences. He recognized I was impressed by his success and he began talking to me about the importance of understanding finances. We talked about the fact that property was the most valuable asset one could have. As a result of those talks, I have always made it my business to try to own properties.

When I reached adulthood and began working, I received a lot of good advice from Jesse. However, the thing I remember most is a conversation we had about the condition of my mother's house. I went to visit her during a rainstorm and was shocked by the condition of the roof of her house. It was literally raining on the inside. The house was old and not well constructed. I knew pouring money into it would be a waste. I called Jesse and told him what I had observed. I proposed to him that I would buy a house for my mother if he would help me with a loan for the down payment. He never hesitated. He said, "Find the house and I will be here for you."

We found a house and put my parents into a much more comfortable environment for the remainder of their lives. JB also finished paying the loan on my mother's car so she would not have that to worry about. I learned a valuable lesson about family during that period.

As time went on, I watched JB become more and more a part of the upper middle class of our society. I became inspired and attempted to achieve a similar lifestyle, while keeping in mind the importance of trying to help others along the way. One thing I can say about JB is no matter how much he gained in life, he always had time to help others achieve success. While he never believed in giving a handout, he was always willing to give a hand up.

To this day, I remain in awe and inspired by Jesse's achievements.

A NOTE FROM ANDRE STRAIN

JB, I am glad to see that you have published a book about your life. Your story and accomplishments are amazing, and I believe people will be blown away by your road to success. You have a passion for helping people, and this book will feed that passion while offering assistance to others. I predict that your book will touch a lot of hands and hearts and inspire people to believe they too can get everything they want out of life with hard work, determination, sheer will and God's lead.

I feel privileged to have had you as an instrumental part of my growth. You have inspired me to reach for more out of life. I have looked up to you since I was 12 years old. Now that I'm a business owner leading my own family, I admire you even more. The advice you have offered me throughout the years has been eerily accurate. You have definitely set a blueprint that if followed, will lead to success just as you have experienced. Your book will no doubt shed light, teach and inspire all who read it. This is a monumental accomplishment.

THANKS FROM YOLONDA

It is not very often that a step-father and a step-daughter build a relationship that mirrors the closeness of blood relatives. JB, I'm thankful for the values and practical knowledge you've taught me over the years. So much of who I've become is largely because you pushed me beyond my limits.

You taught me the value of a dollar, effective planning for the future, and showed me how to really enjoy the fruits of my labor. I play hard because I work hard. I watched you use the same formula over the years. I figured, "Hey, if it works for JB, it should work for me."

I've learned that the tough love I received was in preparation for the tough times I would face as an adult. Although I enjoy an occasional impulsive purchase, I no longer do so without consideration. I make sure I save some money for a rainy day, take care of my immediate responsibilities, and ensure that I have a meal to eat and a place to eat it before randomly buying those brand name shoes at 60% below retail.

Even in my splurging, I know how to find a deal. You taught me the magic of numbers. You taught me that I always have options. You taught me how to plan months down the road before making a decision in the present.

Beyond training me to think more wisely financially, you continued to give me sound advice on living a life with memories I could enjoy later in life rather than regret.

I am blessed because of your care for my future. Thank you, for being a father who invested in my life beyond your covering. Your practical teaching has made my household wealthy in resources. With God's grace and your seeds of wisdom, I am an automatic winner. Thank you, and I love what we've become. Mommy would be proud.

MAXWELL'S INSPIRATION

I remember riding around with Mr. J as a kid as he drove to different locations picking up quarters from arcade machines that he had set up all over

DC. I was just excited to be around video games all of the time; but looking back now I realize the work ethic and pure hustle (in a positive way) this man had. He had everything I could ever dream of as a kid. The Benz, the beautiful house...I loved going to see him because of what he had -- but I had no clue what it took to get those things. Now, I understand.

Mr. J always had a hustler's mentality. Though it sounds cliche', he always stressed that nothing will ever be given to you. You have to go out there and take what you want (legally). Those words resonate every time I feel like things are not going my way. Mr. J is a model of what a man is supposed to be and what many black men tend not to be---consistent and motivated; he consistently motivated me until I got it and I can finally say, "I get it" because of this man. Thank you, Mr. J.

www.ingramcontent.com/pod-product-compliance
Lightning Source LLC
Chambersburg PA
CBHW072009060426
42446CB00042B/2254